GW00836574

SOUTH
STEAM
in the 60s

by Steve McNicol
Photographs by Steve Gradidge

© 1982 by the Publisher:
Railmac Publications
P.O. Box 290, Elizabeth
South Australia 5112

Printed by:
Kitchener Press Pty. Ltd.
Wodonga Street, Beverley,
South Australia 5009

RMPN 18
National Library of Australia Card Number and ISBN
ISBN 0-949817-05-8

At one time the premier express passenger locomotives of the L & S.W.R. the T9 class were still capable of running at high speed in their twilight years. No. 30120 is pictured passing Basingstoke, 28th August 1954.

Almost centenarians and having amassed four million miles between them the three Beattie well tanks were finally replaced on the Wenford Branch during August 1962. They were later used on a special enthusiasts' train and the photograph below shows 30585 and 30587 at Clapham Junction on 2nd December 1962.

CONTENTS

Front cover: The USA class 0-6-0T's were typically American and rather ugly by British standards. No. 30064 is pictured at Guildford, 13th October 1964:

INTRODUCTION

I hope collectors of Railmac Publications will excuse this break from our normal Australasian subjects. The Southern Region (UK) has been a favourite of mine since school days when I used to cycle miles to watch Bulleid Pacifics in action. Living in Frome (Somerset) I was quite handy to the Western Region main line from Paddington to Penzance, the former Somerset & Dorset Joint Railway was only seven miles away at Radstock, Midland locomotives worked into Bristol (25 miles away), but the Southern Region main line was the main drawcard. Semely, Gillingham (Dorset) and Templecombe were all within cycling distance while Salisbury, Yeovil Junction and Weymouth could be reached in a very short time by rail. Other excursions further afield were undertaken, but some of my fondest memories are from those 'close to home' localities.

In writing this book I have endeavoured to include a listing of all Southern locomotives (B.R. Standard types allocated to the Southern have not been included) in service during the early 1960's, a brief history of each type, some technical information as well as a short introduction to the Southern Railway. As the theme is locomotives mainly ¾ portrait views have been used and I sincerely thank Steve Gradidge for supplying the superb photographs to enable me to illustrate this publication.

Southern Steam in the 60's basically follows the format of our Locomotive Series, but being an overseas title it has not been included in that series.

Steve McNicol
January 1982

Rebuilt WC class 4-6-2 No. 34047 Callington, at Yeovil Junction, 27th July 1963. A familiar sight until the Western Region began its diesel invasion of the main line west of Salisbury the following year.

THE SOUTHERN RAILWAY

The Southern Railway came into being when the British Government passed the Railways Act of 1921. This Act effectively amalgamated all railway companies, with the exception of light and industrial lines, into four major groups:

Southern — London & South Western Railway, London Brighton & South Coast Railway and the South Eastern & Chatham Railway.

Western — Great Western Railway, and a number of small Welsh Railways.

North Western, Midland and West Scotland — Midland Railway, London & North Western Railway, Lancashire & Yorkshire Railway, Caledonian Railway, Glasgow & South Western Railway, Highland Railway, North Stafford Railway, Furness Railway.

North Eastern, Eastern and East Scotland — North Eastern Railway, Great Central Railway, Great Northern Railway, Great Eastern Railway, North British Railway, Great North of Scotland Railway.

In addition each of these was to absorb numerous subsidiary companies within their respective territories.

It was not until the 4th January 1923 that the first board meeting of the Southern Railway took place, due to much rivalry between the three main constituent companies.

Under the guidance of Sir Herbert Walker (General Manager 1923-1937, Director 1937-1947), previously General Manager of the L & S.W.R., the pre-grouping companies were gradually moulded into one. During his reign he advocated the commercial exploitation of the Southern Railway's assets and the complete electrification of all suburban lines. He developed the Docks at Southampton and encouraged the Continental services. Although the smallest of the 'Big Four' railway companies the Southern boasted the largest electrified suburban system in the British Isles, if not the world.

The Southern Railway inherited a rather mixed fleet of locomotives of varying sizes and capabilities. A large number were pre-1900 vintage, with some dating as far back as 1872. Each of the three major companies had its own numbering system. The L & S.W.R. numbered its engines between 1 and 773 (with a rather involved duplicate list of locomotives replaced, or with a short working life left), the L.B & S.C.R between 1 and 699 and the S.E & C.R from 1 to 825. This naturally caused some confusion and it was not until 1931, after using a system of letters to denote the railway of origin, that a decision was made to add a prefix to both former S.E & C.R and L.B & S.C.R fleets. The L & S.W.R engines were left as they were, while 1000 was added to the S.E & C.R and 2000 to the L.B & S.C.R.

Over the years the Southern Railway introduced its own locomotives to replace some of the earlier types and under the guidance of R.E.L. Maunsell (Chief Mechanical Engineer 1923-1937) the powerful Lord Nelson class 4-6-0 and highly acclaimed Schools 4-4-0's appeared. With the retirement of Maunsell as C.M.E, Oliver Bulleid was appointed to the position.

Bulleid is perhaps remembered most of all because of his legendary chain driven valve gear fully enclosed in an oil bath (as originally fitted to his Pacifics) and his experimental and ill-fated double ended Leader class, but he played a significant role in the advancement of the Southern Railway's steam locomotive fleet.

SOUTHERN REGION—1962

1 Padstow
2 Wadebridge
3 Bideford
4 Christchurch
5 Lymington
6 Fawley
7 Southampton

8 Cowes
9 Newport
10 Ryde
11 Portsmouth
12 Hayling Island
13 Worthing

14 Shoreham by Sea
15 Hove
16 Brighton
17 Canterbury

18 Faversham
19 Chatham
20 Tonbridge
21 East Grinstead

22 Three Bridges
23 Redhill
24 Dorking
25 Guildford
26 Woking
27 Surbiton

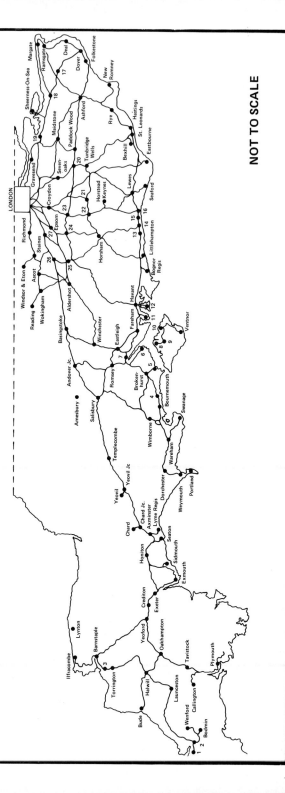

NOT TO SCALE

6

THE SOUTHERN REGION

On the 1st January 1948 the final grouping of main line railways took place and British Railways came into being. The Southern Railway became the Southern Region and its 1,800 steam locomotives were all taken into stock. When renumbering eventually took place, they were listed in the 30000 series. In most cases this only meant the addition of the prefix 3 to their present number. During the interim period the letter 'S' was painted alongside the number to denote a Southern engine.

Despite modernising and upgrading by the Southern Railway a significant number of now ancient locomotives passed into the hands of British Railways. Many of these were still extant in the late 1950's and even the early 1960's.

After extensive trials and locomotive exchanges during 1948 British Railways introduced the first of its standard designs in 1951. These new engines embodied some of the most successful features of pre-grouping engines and dealt the death blow for many non-standard and obsolete classes.

It was not, however, the standard steam locomotives that finally replaced the pre-grouping types, but the internal combustion engine. In 1960 the last steam locomotive was out-shopped from Swindon and at that time there were around 13,000 in traffic. Diesel loco-motives were introduced in such a frenzy that less than eight years later steam propulsion was completely abolished.

The Southern Region had always been keen on electrification and because of this some of its main line types lasted until 1967, when further lines were electrified.

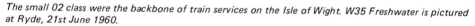

The small 02 class were the backbone of train services on the Isle of Wight. W35 Freshwater is pictured at Ryde, 21st June 1960.

Bulleid's Austerity Q1 class 0-6-0 No. 33003 at Feltham, 8th March 1964. Introduced in 1942 as a wartime measure they were devoid of many superfluous fittings.

An immaculate Rebuilt WC class Pacific No. 34014 Budleigh Salterton, at Eastleigh, 24th March 1963.

CHIEF MECHANICAL ENGINEERS

When describing a locomotive type the name of the Chief Mechanical Engineer who was ultimately responsible for its design is usually mentioned. Each had his own ideas of locomotive construction and during their respective periods in office some special design feature would come to the fore and was later regarded as synonymous with that particular person. Drummond, for instance, fitted a beautifully proportioned chimney with an ornamental flared lip, Bulleid had his boxpok wheels and multi jet blastpipe.

Those C.M.E's mentioned within this book are listed below, roughly in chronological order.

	Railway	Period in office	Noted designs *
J. Beattie	L.S.W.R.	1850-1871	0298 (original)
W. Stroudley	L.B.S.C.R.	1870-1889	A1X, E1
W.G. Beattie	L.S.W.R.	1871-1878	0298
W. Adams	L.S.W.R.	1878-1895	G6, 02, 0415, B4
J. Stirling	S.E.R.	1878-1898	01, R1
R.J. Billinton	L.B.S.C.R.	1890-1904	E4, E6
D. Drummond	L.S.W.R.	1895-1912	M7, T9, 700
H.S. Wainwright	S.E.C.R.	1899-1913	C, D, E, H, L, P
D. Earle Marsh	L.B.S.C.R.	1905-1911	C2X
L.B. Billinton	L.B.S.C.R.	1911-1912	E2, K
R.W. Urie	L.S.W.R.	1912-1922	G16, H15, H16, N15, S15
R.E.L. Maunsell	S.E.C.R.	1913-1922	N, N15 (mod.)
	S.R.	1923-1937	LN, Q, U, V, W, Z
O.V. Bullied	S.R.	1937-1947	MN, BB, WC, Q1

Those surviving into the 1960's.

The Hayling Island branch was the last stronghold of the L.B.S.C.R. 'Terriers' and in this view No. 32678 arrives at Hayling Island, 2nd June 1963.

LOCOMOTIVE DEPOTS

To house its fleet of steam locomotives, the Southern Railway had over 60 depots, of varying size. Those inherited from the L & S.W.R. and sited at strategic locations were large and well equipped (such as Eastleigh, Salisbury and Exmouth Junction). L.B. & S.C.R. depots were generally smaller and more cramped, the major exceptions being some London sites. After the amalgamation of the London Chatham and Dover Railway and the South Eastern Railway around the turn of the century, some rationalisation between these two companies took place. Subsequently those depots that remained in 1923 were well suited and of use to their new owner.

Unlike some other railway companies in the UK, the Southern had very few 'roundhouse' style depots, the notable exceptions being Horsham, Fratton, Guildford and Battersea Park (closed before Nationalisation). Roundhouses were popular in North America, Australia and Europe. Most larger depots were of brick construction but some sub-depots were clad with corrugated iron.

Larger depots such as Eastleigh contained no less than fifteen covered lanes and had an allocation of between 100 and 130 locomotives during Southern days. Other depots with a 100 plus allocation prior to Nationalisation were: Bricklayers Arms, Exmouth Junction, Nine Elms and Stewarts Lane.

Electrification of London suburban lines meant the demise of a number of steam sheds and between 1900 and 1947 no less than ten were either closed or converted to handle electric traction.

Since 1948 others were made redundant by Nationalisation, but a larger number remained until the early 1960's.

Southern Region depots were classified and given a code by British Railways in 1950. The codes were carried on the smokebox doors of locomotives and were on small oblong cast iron plates. The following list is correct for the year 1960 and includes all depots (not just those with a steam allocation). Major depots are in bold type while sub-sheds are allotted the code of the nearest depot with maintenance facilities.

Code	Depot	Code	Depot
70A	**Nine Elms**	71G	Weymouth
70B	Feltham		Bridport
70C	Guildford	71I	Southampton Docks
	Reading South		
70D	Basingstoke	72A	**Exmouth Junction**
70F	Fratton*		Bude, Callington, Exmouth
70H	Ryde		Lyme Regis, Okehampton,
			Seaton
71A	**Eastleigh**	72B	Salisbury
	Andover Junction, Lymington,	72C	Yeovil Town
	Southampton Terminus,	72E	Barnstaple Junction
	Winchester City		Ilfracombe, Torrington
71B	Bournemouth	72F	Wadebridge
	Branksome, Swanage		Launceston

*Although officially closed in November 1959, this depot was still standing in 1960 and was later used to store steam locomotives.

Code	Depot	Code	Depot
73A	**Stewarts Lane**	75A	**Brighton**
73B	Bricklayers Arms		Newhaven, Eastbourne
	Ewer Street	75B	Redhill
73C	Hither Green	75C	Norwood Junction
73E	Faversham	75E	Three Bridges
73F	Ashford		Horsham
	Gillingham (Kent), Ramsgate	75F	Tunbridge Wells West
73H	Dover		
	Folkestone Junction		
73J	Tonbridge		

The former G.W.R. main line from Paddington to the South West had always been in competition with the L & S.W.R.'s route and when the Southern Region west of Salisbury became part of the Western Region during December 1962 it was slowly reduced in status. This also meant that a number of locomotive depots, most of longstanding L & S.W.R. origin, were also transferred. The ultimate indignity.

Those depots involved still retained their allocation of Southern engines, even after being allotted a Western Region code (in September 1963). They became:--

Code	Depot	Code	Depot
83D	Exmouth Junction	83F	Barnstaple Junction
	Bude, Callington, Okehampton,		Torrington, Ilfracombe
	Seaton, Lyme Regis, Exmouth	84E	Wadebridge
83E	Yeovil Town		

A typical shed scene is this one of Tonbridge, 10th June 1961.

The remaining depots (further closures had also taken place due to the withdrawal of additional steam locomotives) were re-coded.

Code	Depot	Code	Depot
70A	Nine Elms	70H	Ryde
70B	Feltham	70I	Southampton Docks
70C	Guildford	73C	Hither Green
	Reading South	73D	St. Leonards
70D	Eastleigh	73E	Faversham
	Andover Junction, Winchester	73F	Ashford
	Southampton Terminus		
70E	Salisbury	75A	Brighton
70F	Bournemouth	75B	Redhill
	Branksome	75C	Norwood Junction
70G	Weymouth	75D	Stewarts Lane
	Bridport	75E	Three Bridges
			Horsham

In July 1965, two years before the end of steam, only eight depots had an allocation of former Southern Railway steam types. They were:— Nine Elms, Feltham, Guildford, Eastleigh, Salisbury, Bournemouth, Weymouth and Ryde. Steam had just about been eliminated in the south east leaving the main lines to Salisbury and Weymouth and those on the Isle of Wight as the last strongholds. Feltham lost its allocation and the Isle of Wight's steam fleet was withdrawn by the end of 1966, but the remainder continued until July 1967.

N class 2-6-0 No. 31841 on a passenger working at Wadebridge, 27th July 1963.

Bulleid's Merchant Navy class were progressively rebuilt from 1956. The end product was an extremely modern and sleek looking machine, as depicted in this photograph of 35027 Port Line, with the Bournemouth Belle at Clapham Junction, 9th March 1964.

LIVERY

The liveries adopted by various railway companies had always been diverse, some choosing rather hideous and unserviceable colours while others had seemingly perfect combinations. The Southern and its pregrouping railways had their share of different liveries.

Dougald Drummond introduced apple green with white, black and chocolate lining on the L & S.W.R. Urie changed the green to sage from 1914 and when Maunsell took over as C.M.E of the S.R. in 1922 he adopted green with yellow lining and lettering for passenger engines. Black, lined dark green was used for goods classes.

At first Bulleid experimented with colours, but eventually settled on a light green with cream and dark green lining for the main line passenger types (LN & V) and an olive green for the other passenger classes. In 1940 he introduced the famous Southern 'Malachite' green although wartime economies stopped any further development and locos were out-shopped unlined black during this period. When hostilities ceased Bulleid again continued with his malachite green with black and white lining.

After Nationalisation B.R. applied its own livery to all engines. For passenger classes, dark green with black and orange lining. Black with red, cream and grey lining for mixed traffic and unlined black for freight and shunting. There were a few exceptions to this rule, including some USA tanks which were painted green lined out in their later years.

For the period of this book the Southern Region's coaching stock was painted a very pleasing shade of mid green. The exception being the Pullman cars, which retained their umber and cream colours.

POWER CLASSIFICATION

To enable easy reference to the capabilities of particular locomotive types a number of codes have been used. Urie introduced a very simple system of letters from A to K, with A denoting the most powerful classes. Some very small locomotives used for specific purposes were not classified at all. British Railways used an alfa-numero coding system. The numbers (from 0 to 9) denoted the power grouping, the greater the power the higher the number. In addition suffixes were used to denote the type of work the locomotives were capable of in that power group, i.e. Passenger or Freight.

Southern Region classes in the 60's were grouped as follows:—

0P	02, A1X, C14, 0298	Unclassed P	
1P	H, 0415	1F	B4
2P	M7, E4	2F	G6, C, E1/T, C2X, E4, 01
3P	T9, D1, E1, L, L1	3F	USA, 700, U, U1, E2, E6
4P	H15, U, N, U1, N1, K	4F	Q
5P	N15, V	5F	H15, N, K, Q1, WC, BB, N1
6P		6F	S15, H16, Z, W
7P	LN, WC, BB	7F	
8P	MN	8F	G16

Some locomotives were given a classification in both categories and were therefore suitable for freight and passenger working. Where a class was equal in both it could be coded as MT.

One of the last workings for Drummond's successful M7 class was the Swanage branch. Here 30052 is observed near Corfe Castle with its push and pull train, 4th May 1963.

Built at Eastleigh in 1936 to a modified design by Maunsell, 30842 was one of the final batch of S15 class 4-6-0's and it is pictured working a local passenger train near Yeovil, 27th July 1963.

SOUTHERN STEAM IN THE 60's

Just under 1,000 locomotives survived into the 60's and there was still a great deal of steam action. But despite this, the end was only seven years away.

A number of expresses were steam hauled and those familiar to the writer included the Atlantic Coast Express, Royal Wessex and the Bournemouth Belle. The A.C.E. in particular as it traversed the main line from London to Exeter and although usually worked by a Merchant Navy it was not uncommon to see one of the lighter Pacifics at the helm. During the summer months relief portions were often run and this sometimes produced some unusual motive power.

Steam could be seen on anything from express passenger to freight and shunting and it was certainly pleasing to be able to turn to an all steam line as others succumbed to the throb of the diesel engine.

In the following pages all steam locomotives (BR and 'foreign' types are excluded) in service on the Southern Region during the Spring of 1960 are listed together with historical notes and technical information. Most classes are illustrated. As this book is designed for the Australian market only basic information is given. There are a number of more comprehensive works available from British publishers for those wanting in depth studies of particular types. There is also a slight bias towards the L & S.W.R. and S.R., for obvious reasons, and I hope I am forgiven if I over indulge when describing some classes.

Note: Imperial measurements have been used throughout this publication as all locomotives were built before the introduction of metrication in Australia.

Dugald Drummond's M7 class entered traffic from March 1897 and were put to work on semi-fast passenger trains throughout the system. However, one of the class derailed at speed in 1898 and they were subsequently relegated to London suburban and some short cross country passenger workings. As the electrification of the suburban network increased so more and more became allotted to country depots.

From 1912 a number of M7's were fitted for push and pull working on country branches, but in 1930 the first locomotives received the more sophisticated compressed air auto train equipment used on some L.B. & S.C.R. engines. In 1921 one of the class was superheated and although it was evidently considered successful no others were similarly modified.

When taken into B.R. stock the M7 class had penetrated almost all of the former L & S.W.R. territory and even into neighbouring L.B. & S.C.R. lines. They were used extensively for branch passenger trains and for shunting. Their final duties were on the Lymington and Swanage push and pull services, as well as shunting at Salisbury, and the last nine were all withdrawn from service in May 1964.

Introduced	: 1897	Builder	: L & S.W.R.		
Pressure	: 175lb sq in	No. built	: 105		
Cylinders	: 18½in x 26in	Weight	: 60tons 4cwt		
T.E.	: 19,756lb		60tons 3cwt*		
Driving wheel	: 5ft 7in		62tons 0cwt†		
Trailing wheel	: 3ft 7in	Length	: 35ft 0¼in		
Extended frames *			36ft 3in*†		
Push and Pull fitted†		Total	: 73		

30021†	30040	30057†	30112	30247	30377*
30023	30043	30058†	30124*	30248	30378*
30024	30044	30059†	30125†	30249	30379†
30025	30045†	30060†	30127*	30251	30479*
30028†	30048†	30104†	30128†	30253	30480†
30029†	30049†	30105†	30129†	30254*	30667
30031	30050†	30106†	30131†	30255	30668
30032	30051†	30107†	30132*	30320	30669
30033	30052†	30108†	30133†	30321	30670
30034	30053†	30109†	30241	30328†	30673
30035	30055†	30110†	30245	30357	30674
30036	30056†	30111†	30246	30375*	30676
30039					

0-6-0T   **USA**   **SR**

This small group of locomotives was built from 1942 but not purchased until December 1946. They were a standard U.S. Army design and had to be fitted with a modified cab, bunker, and other minor alterations before entering service. They proved extremely useful as a heavy duty shunting locomotive and spent most of their life in and around Southampton Docks, although a few were later employed further afield after dieselisation of the docks.

Six were eventually taken into Departmental stock and two received names (*Maunsell* and *Wainwright*). They lasted well into the 60's and were one of the last Southern steam types in service.

M7 class 0-4-4T No. 30254, near Brockenhurst, 14th September 1963 (extended frames).

USA class 0-6-0T No. 30070, Eastleigh, 4th May 1963

Introduced	: 1946	Builder	: Vulcan (USA)
Pressure	: 210lb sq in	No. built	: 14
Cylinders	: 16½in x 24in	Weight	: 46tons 10cwt
T.E.	: 21,598lb	Length	: 29ft 8in
Driving wheel	: 4ft 6in	Total	: 14

30061	30064	30067	30069	30071	30073
30062	30065	30068	30070	30072	30074
30063	30066				

0-4-0T   B4   LSWR

The miniature B4 class were introduced by William Adams for light dock shunting and pilot duties. The first few were constructed at Nine Elms and allocated to Exmouth Junction, Salisbury, Northam and Bournemouth. But shortly afterwards a further ten were built for use in Southampton Docks. Dugald Drummond introduced his version of the B4 (classified K14) in 1908. Those engines working in Southampton Docks were given names, but these were removed later in their life.

With the arrival of the heavier USA tanks the B4's were gradually withdrawn from the docks and a number were sold to private industry. The first to be withdrawn was No. 176 in June 1948, closely followed by another thirteen. The remainder were given lesser duties such as shed pilots and only four survived in 1960. 30093 was withdrawn in April 1960 but the others remained as shed pilots at Guildford and Winchester before finally being replaced between March and October 1963.

Introduced	: 1891	Builder	: L & S.W.R.
Pressure	: 140lb sq in	No. built	· : 25
Cylinders	: 16in x 22in	Weight	: 33tons 9 cwt
T.E.	: 14,649lb	Length	: 24ft 10½in
Driving wheel	: 3ft 9¾in	Total	: 4

30089	30093	30096	30102

4-4-0   T9   LSWR

Dugald Drummond made a number of improvements to the design of the C8 class 4-4-0's to increase performance and efficiency. Subsequently the first of the successful T9 class entered traffic in February 1899. They soon earned the nickname *Greyhounds* because of their seemingly effortless ease when working light passenger trains.

A number of alterations were made during their life, the most signifcant being the fitting of superheated boilers between 1923 and 1929. This even further enhanced their performance and there are many legendary high speed runs behind a T9.

As the size and weight of the express passenger trains increased they were replaced on these prestigious workings by larger 4-6-0's but still remained on passenger trains. The first was withdrawn in 1951 but the majority followed shortly afterwards, and the last was taken out of regular service during 1961. No. 30120 was retained for preservation and fully restored during 1962/3, being used on a number of special excursions before being placed in storage.

B4 class 0-4-0T No. 30089, Guildford, 5th June 1960.

T9 class 4-4-0 No. 30120, Eastleigh, 28th August 1954.

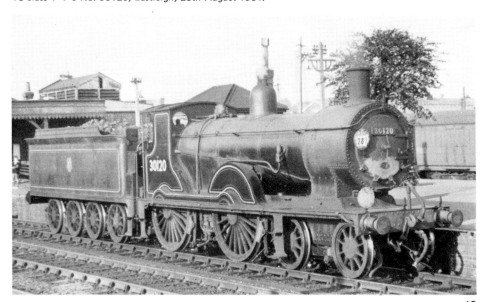

Introduced	: 1899	Builder	: Dubs and L & S.W.R.
Pressure	: 175lb sq in	No. built	: 66
Cylinders	: 19in x 26in	Weight	: 96tons 3cwt (average)
T.E.	: 17,673lb	Length	: 63ft 9in (8-w tender)
Driving wheel	: 6ft 7in	Total	: 14
Bogie wheel	: 3ft 7in		

30117	30288	30338	30709	30717	30719
30120	30300	30707	30715	30718	30729
30287	30313				

0-4-4T   02   LSWR

The first 02 class entered traffic in December 1889 and by the year 1895 all sixty were in service. They were basically a smaller version of Adams T1 class and were designed for light suburban services, as well as for short branch line work. Like the M7's some received the push and pull equipment.

The first 02 was fitted with Westinghouse air brake and transferred to the Isle of Wight in May 1923 and by April 1949 a total of twenty three had been so treated. All were renumbered into I.O.W. stock and later named. They were also given extended coal bunkers from 1932*.

During their lives they were reboilered (some with a rather unsuccessful design by Drummond) and numerous other modifications took place. The first was withdrawn in 1933 and by 1960 the majority of the survivors were working on the Isle of Wight.

Introduced	: 1889	Builder	: L & S.W.R.
Pressure	: 160lb sq in	No. built	: 60
Cylinders	: 17½in x 24in	Weight	: 46tons 18cwt
T.E.	: 17,234lb		48tons 8cwt*
Driving wheel	: 4ft 10in		49tons 12cwt†*
Trailing wheel	: 3ft	Length	: 30ft 8½in
			30ft 11in*
Push and Pull fitted † (W35, W36)		Total	: 27

30183	30193	30200	30223	30225	30229
30192	30199				

W14 Fishbourne	W24 Calbourne	W30 Shorwell
W16 Ventnor	W25 Godshill	W31 Chale
W17 Seaview	W26 Whitwell	W32 Bonchurch
W18 Ningwood	W27 Merstone	W33 Bembridge
W20 Shanklin	W28 Ashey	W35 Freshwater
W21 Sandown	W29 Alverstone	W36 Carisbrooke
W22 Brading		

0-6-0T   G6   LSWR

Apart from the wheel arrangement the Adams G6 class was similar to the 02. The first ten were delivered during 1894 and put to work on shunting and local goods activities. When some of the B4's were transferred from country depots to Southampton Docks further G6 class were ordered to replace them.

T9 class 4-4-0 No. 30724, Basingstoke, 28th August 1954 (withdrawn in May 1959).

O2 class 0-4-4T No. 30199, Eastleigh, 4th May 1963.

Drummond continued building the class until a total of thirty-four was reached in 1900. In their early years they could also be observed banking trains between Exeter St. Davids and Central, until replaced by larger locomotives.

When Nationalisation came, a number of reconditioned E4 class 0-6-2T's were introduced to the former L & S.W.R. system to replace some of the G6 class which, at that stage, were in very run down condition. Over the next few years twenty-three were condemned and one transferred to service stock for shunting Meldon Quarry. Condemnations continued in the late 1950's and only seven locomotives survived past 1960. The last two in general service were withdrawn in July 1961, followed by the service locomotive (30238 had been transferred to departmental stock in November 1960 to replace DS3152, which was then withdrawn) in December 1962.

Introduced	: 1894	Builder	: L & S.W.R.		
Pressure	: 160lb sq in	No. built	: 34		
Cylinders	: 17½in x 24in	Weight	: 47tons 13cwt		
T.E.	: 17,234lb	Length	: 30ft 8½in		
Driving wheel	: 4ft 10in	Total	: 7		

30238	30258	30266	30274	30277	30349
DS3152 (30272)					

0-6-0   700   LSWR

One of Dugald Drummond's first actions on arrival in the south was to seek quotations for a new tender locomotive. The order was placed with Dubs & Co. and by March 1897 delivery had commenced. They were primarily intended for freight working but saw some use on light passenger trains.

In 1920 Urie decided to modernise one of the 700 class by rebuilding it with an extended smokebox, capuchon capped stove pipe chimney, new firebox and an Eastleigh superheater. The boiler barrel was also raised and the frames lengthened. The rest of the class were similarly treated between 1921 and 1929, although Maunsell superheaters were adopted in later rebuilds. All of the 700 class were eventually fitted with Maunsell superheaters.

Withdrawals did not commence until September 1957, after 30688 was involved in a collision and only one other followed prior to 1960. However they were rapidly replaced during 1961 and 1962. 30368 was the last withdrawn, in December 1962, but two or three saw limited service after this date on snow plough duties.

Introduced	: 1897	Builder	: Dubs & Co.		
Pressure	: 180lb sq in	No. built	: 30		
Cylinders	: 19in x 26in	Weight	: 83tons 8cwt		
T.E.	: 23,542lb	Length	: 54ft 1¼in		
Driving wheel	: 5ft 1in	Total	: 28		

30306	30317	30346	30689	30694	30698
30308	30325	30350	30690	30695	30699
30309	30326	30355	30691	30696	30700
30315	30327	30368	30692	30697	30701
30316	30339	30687	30693		

G6 class 0-6-0T No. 30349, Feltham, 8th January 1961.

700 class 0-6-0 No. 30689, Feltham, 8th January 1961.

The H15 was Robert Urie's first design for the L & S.W.R. after his appointment as Chief Mechanical Engineer in 1912. A two cylinder mixed traffic 4-6-0, the first entered traffic in 1914 and the rest of the initial batch of ten later that year. Eight were fitted with superheaters (four each Schmidt or Robinson types) to evaluate their effectiveness. The Robinson design was evidently the more successful of the two and with a few alterations Urie later re-introduced it as the standard Eastleigh superheater.

Further locomotives, with minor modifications (including Maunsell's design of super-heater), were ordered new from 1923 while earlier Drummond 4-6-0's of the solitary E14 and F13 classes were rebuilt along the lines of the H15. Maunsell made further alterations to the later series, including the replacement of the stove pipe chimney with one of his own design, and the fitting of smoke deflectors during the 1929-31 period in an effort to keep the exhaust smoke clear of the footplate.

They were employed mainly on the West of England main line and to Portsmouth and Bournemouth, hauling semi-fast passenger and fast goods services. Trials were made in the eastern section, though not very successfully. Withdrawals commenced in 1955 and the bulk of the class was out of traffic by 1960. The last four were withdrawn in December 1961.

Introduced	: 1914	Builder	: L & S.W.R. and SR		
Pressure	: 180lb sq in	No. built	: 26 (incl. rebuilds)		
	175lb sq in*	Weight	: 129tons 14cwt*		
Cylinders	: 21in x 28in		136tons 7cwt		
T.E.	: 26,240lb		137tons 9cwt†		
	25,511lb*	Length	: 65ft 6¾in (approx)		
Driving wheel	: 6ft	Total	: 10		
Bogie wheel	: 3ft 7in				

F13 class 4,300 gal. tender (others 5,000 gal.)

Early series (Urie)†

30331*	30475	30489†	30521	30523	30524
30474	30476	30491†	30522		

4-6-0   N15   LSWR

The N15, more commonly referred to as the King Arthur class, were built to supplement the L & S.W.R.'s fleet of passenger locomotives. Urie designed and ordered the initial batch of ten in 1916 but because of material shortages due to the war the first did not enter traffic until August 1918. Although many parts were similar to the mixed traffic H15's the boiler barrel was tapered, a departure from standard L & S.W.R. practice. Another ten were ordered in 1920, the last three being delivered after the 1923 railway grouping.

From the outset the N15's were assigned to the more glamorous express passenger workings mainly on the London to Exeter main line. They were reasonably successful on these duties and when Maunsell looked for further 4-6-0's he perpetuated the N15 design, but not before carrying out extensive trials to find ways to increase their efficiency.

H15 class 4-6-0 No. 30477, Eastleigh, 28th August 1954.

Urie N15 class 4-6-0 No. 30737 King Uther (with multi-jet blast pipe and large diameter chimney), Basingstoke, 28th August 1954. (Withdrawn 1956)

In all seventy-four locomotives were constructed, twenty by Urie at Eastleigh and fifty-four by Maunsell (24 at Eastleigh and 30 by the North British Locomotive Co.). They differed slightly between batches and a number of modifications to individual engines took place over the years.

Some N15's later found their way to the eastern section depots while during 1942/3 ten of the class were loaned to the London North Eastern Railway where they saw service, mainly on fast goods trains, but also on some passenger workings.

A large amount of tender swapping took place on the Southern Railway, but unfortunately space precludes going into any great detail. It would suffice to say that during their life various types of tenders, both new and secondhand, were fitted to the N15 class.

Naming of the whole class commenced in 1925 and smoke deflectors were added shortly afterwards.

The first N15 was withdrawn in 1955 and all of Urie's engines were gone by March 1958. The remainder survived into the 1960's but were withdrawn by November 1962.

Introduced	: 1918	Builder	: L & S.W.R. and N.B.L.
Pressure	: 200lb sq in	No. built	: 74
Cylinders	: 20½in x 28in	Weight	: 138tons 10cwt (approx.)
T.E.	: 25,321lb		123tons 2cwt*
Driving wheel	: 6ft 7in	Length	: 66ft 5¼in (average)
Bogie wheel	: 3ft 7in	Total	: 34

30794/99/804 with 6 wheel 3,500 gallon tender for eastern section. Others 5,000 gallons.*

30448	Sir Tristram	30781	Sir Aglovale
30450	Sir Kay	30782	Sir Brian
30451	Sir Lamorak	30783	Sir Gillemere
30453	King Arthur	30788	Sir Urre of the Mount
30456	Sir Galahad	30790	Sir Villiars
30457	Sir Bedivere	30791	Sir Uwaine
30763	Sir Bors de Ganis	30793	Sir Ontzlake
30764	Sir Gawain	30794	Sir Ector de Maris
30765	Sir Gareth	30795	Sir Dinadan
30768	Sir Balin	30796	Sir Dodinas le Savage
30769	Sir Balan	30798	Sir Hectimere
30770	Sir Prianius	30799	Sir Ironside
30771	Sir Sagramore	30800	Sir Meleaus de Lile
30772	Sir Percivale	30802	Sir Durnore
30773	Sir Lavaine	30803	Sir Harry le Fise Lake
30775	Sir Agravaine	30804	Sir Cador of Cornwall
30777	Sir Lamiel	30806	Sir Galleron

4-8-0T   G16   LSWR

With the construction of a marshalling yard at Feltham a new powerful locomotive was required to propel the wagons over the 'hump' where they were gravity fed into their respective sidings. Four large 4-8-0T's, designed in 1916 but not ordered from Eastleigh until 1918, entered traffic in 1921.

Maunsell N15 class 4-6-0 No. 30772 Sir Percivale, Eastleigh, 14th May 1960.

G16 class 4-8-0T No. 30494, Feltham, 29th October 1961.

Designed for a specific purpose, which they capably performed, the G16 class spent nearly all of their lives shunting at Feltham. Only minor modifications were deemed necessary during their 40 years of service although new and reconditioned boilers and Maunsell superheaters were fitted from 1928.

The first two were withdrawn in 1959 and the rest in 1962.

Introduced	:	1921	Builder	:	L & S.W.R.
Pressure	:	180lb sq in	No. built	:	4
Cylinders	:	22in x 28in	Weight	:	95tons 2cwt
T.E.	:	33,991lb	Length	:	42ft 10¼in
Driving wheel	:	5ft 1in	Total	:	2
Bogie wheel	:	3ft 7in			

30494   30495

4-6-0	S15	LSWR

Considered a 'goods' version of the N15 class, having smaller driving wheels, the S15 class were nevertheless a very versatile and successful locomotive. Robert Urie was responsible for their design and the first was outshopped from Eastleigh in March 1920 with all twenty locomotives in traffic by May 1921.

Maunsell made only slight modifications when he ordered another ten engines in May 1926, five more in July of the same year, followed by the final series of ten locomotives in January 1936.

In February 1921 experiments were undertaken with one locomotive as it was fitted with a modified blastpipe and chimney. The tests being successful others were altered in a similar manner. The Urie engines were fitted with Maunsell superheaters between 1927 and 1931 and U1 chimneys between 1936 and 1948. A variety of tenders were fitted over the years with varying water capacities.

Maunsell brought some degree of standardisation to the railway, especially with the S15, N15 and Southern Railway H15's having interchangeable boilers. They were all fitted with smoke deflectors later in life and although intended for goods train working they were commonly seen on passenger services, especially in the West Country.

In 1960 all forty-five were still in active service and the first was not withdrawn until as late as November 1962, with the last five surviving until September 1965.

Introduced	:	1920	Builder	:	L & S.W.R. and S.R.
Pressure	:	180lb sq in	No. built	:	45
		200lb sq in*†	Weight	:	137tons 9 cwt
Cylinders	:	21in x 28in			137tons 2cwt*
		20½in x 28in*†			138tons 1cwt†
T.E.	:	28,198lb	Length	:	65ft 6¾in (approx)
		29,856lb*†	Total	:	45
Driving wheel	:	5ft 7in			
Bogie wheel	:	3ft 7in			

*NB: All weights are original. Maunsell *, final Maunsell series†.*

Urie S15 class 4-6-0 No. 30498, Eastleigh, 2nd June 1963.

Maunsell (final series) S15 class 4-6-0 No. 30840, Feltham, 13th October 1964.

30496	30504	30512	30827*	30834*	30841†
30497	30505	30513	30828*	30835*	30842†
30498	30506	30514	30829*	30836*	30843†
30499	30507	30515	30830*	30837*	30844†
30500	30508	30823*	30831*	30838†	30845†
30501	30509	30824*	30832*	30839†	30846†
30502	30510	30825*	30833*	30840†	30847†
30503	30511	30826*			

4-6-2T   H16   LSWR

Similar in most respects to the G16 class these five 4-6-2 tanks were introduced for short transfer working between major goods yards in the London area. They did see some limited use on other duties including Ascot race specials and empty stock workings out of Waterloo.

Like the G16's they received few alterations, but during 1928-29 a Maunsell superheater was fitted to replace Urie's earlier Eastleigh type.

In the early 1960's they ventured further afield to handle the Fawley branch oil trains until displaced by the W class. After returning to Feltham they soon became redundant and were all withdrawn during 1962.

Introduced	: 1921	Builder	:	L & S.W.R.
Pressure	: 180lb sq in	No. built	:	5
Cylinders	: 21in x 28in	Weight	:	98tons 8cwt
T.E.	: 28,198lb	Length	:	46ft
Driving wheel	: 5ft 7in	Total	:	5
Bogie wheel	: 3ft 7in			

30516	30517	30518	30519	30520

0-6-0   Q   SR

A neat and powerful 0-6-0, the first of the Q class entered traffic in January 1938. They were designed by Maunsell just prior to his retirement and were intended to replace earlier light mixed traffic locomotives. They retained many Maunsell features such as Belpaire firebox, side window cab, snifting valves on smokebox top and chimney. New tenders were constructed at the same time, but these were given to larger locomotives and the Q's were subsequently fitted with secondhand U class 3,500 gallon tenders.

Various alterations were made to their blastpipe and chimney, firstly by Bulleid (Lemaitre multiple jet blastpipe and large diameter chimney fitted between 1940 and 1949) and later by British Railways (from 1955).

In their twilight years the Q class were relegated to local goods and shunting work, while some were fitted with snow ploughs in the winter months. The first was withdrawn in November 1962 and the last by mid 1965.

H16 class 4-6-2T No. 30520, Feltham, 15th September 1962.

Q class 0-6-0 No. 30548, Eastleigh, 28th August 1954.

Introduced	: 1938	Builder	: S.R.
Pressure	: 200lb sq in	No. built	: 20
Cylinders	: 19in x 26in	Weight	: 90tons
T.E.	: 26,158lb	Length	: 53ft 9½in
Driving wheel	: 5ft 1in	Total	: 20

30530	30534	30538	30541	30544	30547
30531	30535	30539	30542	30545	30548
30532	30536	30540	30543	30546	30549
30533	30537				

4-4-2T	0415	LSWR

These beautifully proportioned locomotives were a legacy from that grand era of rail-roading when locomotives were designed to please the onlooker as well as capably per-forming their daily tasks. The first 0415 entered traffic in August 1882 and was built by Beyer Peacock & Co., from drawings supplied by W. Adams. Further locomotives were constructed by no less than four different manufacturers (Dubs & Co, R. Stephenson, Neilson & Co, and Beyer Peacock)* and by 1885 all seventy-one were in traffic. Some of the later locomotives had minor variations, including slightly larger water tanks.

They were put to work on London suburban services although a handful could be seen in North Devon. During the early 1900's a few more were transferred into the country and some even fitted for push and pull working. The T1 class suburban tanks and electrifica-tion finally ousted them from the London metropolitan area and by 1922, nine had been withdrawn (although large numbers were laid aside at Eastleigh some years earlier). This increased to fifty by 1925 and sixty-nine by 1928.

The two survivors (by this time numbered 0125 and 0520 in the duplicate list) were to be found working the Lyme Regis branch until 1928 when Maunsell experimented with other small locomotive types, albeit unsuccessfully. Their flexible wheelbase was ideal for this sharply curved branch line and they were subsequently overhauled and returned to service.

In 1946, when the two survivors (since renumbered 3125 and 3520) were again due for heavy repairs, the Southern Railway realised the need for an additional engine and they approached the Kent & East Sussex Railway to try and purchase their number 5 (formerly L & S.W.R. No. 0488 but sold to K & E.S.R. in 1917). It became the property of the Southern in March 1946 and, after overhaul, joined the other two on the Lyme Regis branch.

All three survived Nationalisation and were renumbered 30582 to 30584 (3125, 3488 and 3520 respectively) in British Railways stock. They remained on the branch until 1960 when the track was upgraded and re-aligned to permit the use of more modern engines. All three were withdrawn between January and July 1961, but luckily No. 30583 was purchased for preservation by the Bluebell Railway.

Introduced	: 1882	Builder	: Various*
Pressure	: 160lb sq in	No. built	: 71
Cylinders	: 17½in x 24in	Weight	: 55tons 2cwt (average)
Driving wheel	: 5ft 7in	T.E.	: 14,919lb
Bogie wheel	: 3ft	Total	: 3

30582	30583	30584

0415 class 4-4-2T No. 30583, Axminster, 25th June 1960.

0415 class 4-4-2T No 488 (30583), Sheffield Park, 1st April 1962 (restored to L & S.W.R. livery).

Joseph Beattie, in close liaison with Beyer Peacock & Co., introduced a small neat 2-4-0WT in 1863. Beattie's son William continued with the construction of further engines until by 1875 a total of eighty-five were in traffic. At that time the 2-4-0 wheel arrangement was quite popular for passenger locomotives and the 0298 class was considered an improved version of earlier L & S.W.R. types. They worked on the London suburban system and were only displaced by the advent of larger and more powerful locomotives after giving around twenty years' service.

The Beattie well tanks could then be seen working at various country locations, being used for shunting and branch line work. But withdrawals soon commenced, and all but three had been taken out of active service by the end of 1899.

The three survivors were placed on the duplicate list and numbered 0298, 0314 and 0329 and worked exclusively on the lightly laid Wenford Bridge branch line, mainly on china clay traffic. They remained on this line all of their lives and were rebuilt on a number of occasions by Drummond, Urie and later by Maunsell. Their appearance naturally changed over the years with their rather spartan open cabs being one of the first alterations. The original slender copper capped chimney was replaced by an Adams stove pipe, but during a later rebuild they reverted to a more conventional Drummond pattern chimney. A number of different boilers were fitted, including brand new ones built at Eastleigh and of Drummond style (with safety valves mounted on the dome) during the latter half of 1921. Maunsell also had new front ends fitted to the frames and this included replacing the leading timber buffer beam with one constructed of steel.

On entering British Railways stock they became 30585 to 30587 (0314, 0329 and 0298 respectively) and in 1960 were still hard at work. 30586 differed slightly from the other two in having large square splashers, from a distance looking somewhat like small water tanks. In August 1962 three small Western Region '1366' class pannier tanks were found to be suitable replacements and the Beatties finally retired. Shortly afterwards 30586 was observed by the writer parked in a siding at Yeovil Town, but the other two returned to London after an absence of over 60 years to work a farewell passenger train. All three were officially withdrawn in December that year.

Introduced	: 1863	Builder	: Beyer Peacock
Pressure	: 160lb sq in	No. built	: 85
Cylinders	: 16½in x 22in	Weight	: 35tons 15cwt (average)
T.E.	: 12,158lb	Length	: 26ft 2in
Driving wheel	: 5ft 7in	Total	: 3
Leading wheel	: 3ft 7¾in		

30585   30586   30587

4-6-0   LN   SR

In 1926 Maunsell introduced a large four cylindered express passenger locomotive for working the heavy Continental boat trains between Victoria and Dover. They became known as the Lord Nelson class and by the end of 1929 all sixteen were in service.

Their design was somewhat unusual in that the driving axle cranks were set at 135° instead of the normal 90°, which meant the engine gave eight beats per revolution of the driving wheel as against the usual four.

0298 class 2-4-0WT No. 30585, Eastleigh, 18th September 1960.

LN class 4-6-0 No. 30855 Robert Blake, Eastleigh, 14th May 1960.

They were a rather solid looking machine and with their large boilers dwarfed all other locomotives on the Southern Railway. When built they did not have smoke deflectors, but these were fitted after only a few years' service. Ten of the class also received S15 tenders and they were all rebuilt from 1937 with higher sides.

Bulleid made a number of modifications from 1938 including the fitting of new cylinders, multi-jet blastpipe and large diameter chimney, to improve their performance.

In the mid 1950's they were allocated to Eastleigh, Bournemouth and Nine Elms sheds, working heavy passenger trains to Southampton Docks and Bournemouth. They were sometimes found further afield, and 30859 was observed in Western Region territory late in 1961 stabled at Westbury depot. By 1962 the dozen or so survivors were allocated to Eastleigh, but all were withdrawn by the end of the year.

Introduced	: 1926	Builder	:	S.R.
Pressure	: 220lb sq in	No. built	:	16
Cylinders	: (4) 16½ x 26in	Weight	:	142tons 6cwt (approx.)
T.E.	: 33,511lb			143tons 12cwt†
	35,298lb*	Length	:	69ft 9¾in
Driving wheel	: 6ft 7in	Bogie wheel	:	3ft 1in
	6ft 3in*	Total	:	16

Smaller diameter wheels*, longer boiler†, conventional 4-beat exhaust‡.

30850	Lord Nelson	30858	Lord Duncan
30851	Sir Francis Drake	30859	Lord Hood*
30852	Sir Walter Raleigh	30860	Lord Hawke†
30853	Sir Richard Grenville	30861	Lord Anson
30854	Howard of Effingham	30862	Lord Collingwood
30855	Robert Blake	30863	Lord Rodney
30856	Lord St. Vincent	30864	Sir Martin Frobisher
30857	Lord Howe	30865	Sir John Hawkins‡

4-4-0   V   SR

Maunsell's final passenger design, the V or 'Schools' class, was introduced in 1930 to handle express passenger trains on the South Eastern section, especially the Hastings line which had a restricted loading gauge. After the initial batch of ten locomotives a further five entered traffic in 1932, ten in 1933 and the final fifteen during 1934-35. They were the last 4-4-0 designed in England and by far the most powerful.

Considered by many as a smaller version of the LN class they were very similar, with the most noticeable differences being the wheelbase, the use of three cylinders instead of four, and round topped firebox in place of the more square Belpair style. Like the LN class they also received smoke deflectors early in their lives and from 1938 about half of the class were fitted with a multi-jet blastpipe and large diameter chimney*.

In later years they were also gainfully employed between Waterloo and Bournemouth and in fact replaced the older King Arthur (N15) class 4-6-0's on a number of trains.

LN class 4-6-0 No. 30864 Sir Martin Frobisher, Eastleigh, 14th May 1960.

V class 4-4-0 No. 30900 Eton, Tonbridge, 23rd March 1957. (Multi-jet blast pipe and large diameter chimney.)

Nine Elms, Guildford and Basingstoke all had an allocation of Schools class by 1962, and during the summer of that year 30925 was observed working a relief portion of the Atlantic Coast Express at Chard Junction. All were withdrawn by the end of 1962.

Introduced	:	1930	Builder	:	S.R.
Pressure	:	220lb sq in	No. built	:	40
Cylinders	:	(3) 16½in x 26in	Weight	:	109tons 10cwt
T.E.	:	25,133lb	Length	:	58ft 9¾in
Driving wheel	:	6ft 7in	Total	:	40
Bogie wheel	:	3ft 1in			

*Fitted with multi-jet blastpipe *.*

30900	Eton*	30920	Rugby*
30901	Winchester*	30921	Shrewsbury*
30902	Wellington	30922	Marlborough
30903	Charterhouse	30923	Bradfield
30904	Lancing	30924	Haileybury*
30905	Tonbridge	30925	Cheltenham
30906	Sherborne	30926	Repton
30907	Dulwich*	30927	Clifton
30908	Westminster	30928	Stowe
30909	St. Pauls*	30929	Malvern*
30910	Merchant Taylors	30930	Radley*
30911	Dover	30931	King's Wimbledon*
30912	Downside	30932	Blundells
30913	Christ's Hospital*	30933	King's Canterbury*
30914	Eastbourne*	30934	St. Lawrence*
30915	Brighton*	30935	Sevenoaks
30916	Whitgift	30936	Cranleigh
30917	Ardingly*	30937	Epsom*
30918	Hurstpierpoint*	30938	St. Olave's*
30919	Harrow*	30939	Leatherhead*

0-8-0T   Z   SR

In March 1929 there emerged from Brighton workshops the first of a small class of heavy duty shunting locomotives. Designed by Maunsell they were slightly shorter than the earlier Urie G16 and H16 classes although of similar power and with no bogie or trailing wheels they had a rather long overhang at each end. Three cylinders were provided, and this considerably reduced the noise from their exhaust.

In January 1947 the class was allocated as follows: 950/1/3/5/6 Hither Green, 952 Eastleigh, 954 Exmouth Junction and 957 at Salisbury. Hither Green had lost its allocation by 1955 as they were relocated amongst eastern section sheds and also Templecombe. However, their final years were spent at Exmouth Junction where two locomotives at a time could be seen banking trains between Exeter St. Davids and Central. All were withdrawn by the end of 1962.

Introduced	:	1929	Builder	:	S.R.
Pressure	:	180lb sq in	No. built	:	8
Cylinders	:	(3) 16in x 28in	Weight	:	71tons 12 cwt

V class 4-4-0 No. 30917 Ardingly, Eastleigh, 24th March 1963 (multi-jet blastpipe and large diameter chimney).

V class 4-4-0 No. 30904 Lancing, near Nine Elms, 21st September 1957

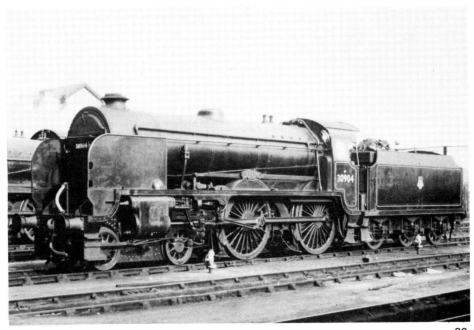

T.E.	: 29,376lb	Length	: 39ft 4in
Driving wheel	: 4ft 8in	Total	: 8

30950	30952	30954	30955	30956	30957
30951	30953				

0-6-0   C   SECR

Just prior to the merger of the L.C. & D.R. and the S.E.R. moves were afoot to construct additional 0-6-0 goods engines for the L.C. & D.R. On taking office in the newly formed S.E. & C.R., Harry Wainwright immediately invited tenders for the supply of a new goods engine. The first entered traffic in 1900 and Ashford workshops, Sharp, Stewart & Co., Longhedge workshops and Neilson Reid & Co., all contributed until by 1908 a total of one hundred and nine were in service.

They remained basically unaltered throughout their life, but some modifications to individual locomotives took place, including the conversion of 31592 to a saddle tank for a number of years.

The C class could be found scattered all over the L.C. & D.R. on goods workings, but just before the grouping the larger N class 2-6-0 had made inroads into their main line duties. In later years they could be observed more often working branch and light goods turns as well as local passenger trains in the south east.

The first two were withdrawn in 1947 but the rest entered B.R. stock. By spring 1960 forty-eight had been taken out of traffic and the remainder were to disappear over the next three years. 31271, 31280 and 31592 were transferred to service stock for shunting Ashford wagon works and were not written off until the mid 1960's.

Introduced	: 1900	Builder	: Various
Pressure	: 160lb sq in	No. built	: 109
Cylinders	: 18½in x 26in	Weight	: 82tons 1cwt
T.E.	: 19,519lb	Length	: 51ft 7½in
Driving wheel	: 5ft 2in	Total	: 61

31004	31223	31287	31575	31684	31715
31037	31229	31293	31578	31686	31716
31054	31242	31298	31579	31689	31717
31061	31244	31317	31583	31690	31719
31068	31255	31480	31584	31691	31720
31086	31256	31481	31588	31692	31721
31102	31267	31495	31589	31693	31722
31112	31268	31498	31590	31694	31723
31113	31271	31510	31592	31695	31724
31150	31280	31573	31682	31714	31725
31218					

0-4-4T   H   SECR

The H class were developed by Wainwright as a replacement for some of the older tank classes working in the London area.

Z class 0-8-0T No. 30957, Exmouth Junction, 27th July 1961.

C class 0-6-0 No. 31692, Ashford, 16th April 1960.

Ashford constructed the first locomotive in 1904 and a further six entered traffic later that year. The last two arrived in 1915 and by then the class had reached its peak of sixty-six.

They could be found working passenger trains on most parts of the former S.E.R. system after electrification of some suburban services in 1925-26, and from 1949 a number were fitted with push and pull apparatus*.

The first was withdrawn in 1944 but the majority of the class lasted into the 50's with the final engine, No. 31263, being condemned in January 1964.

Introduced	: 1904	Builder	: S.E. & C.R.		
Pressure	: 160lb sq in	No. built	: 66		
Cylinders	: 18in x 26in	Weight	: 54tons 8cwt		
T.E.	: 17,359lb	Length	: 33ft		
Driving wheel	: 5ft 6in	Total	: 37		
Trailing wheel	: 3ft 7in				

31005*	31265	31307	31328	31520*	31543*
31161*	31266*	31308*	31500*	31521*	31544*
31162*	31276*	31310*	31512*	31522*	31550
31177*	31278*	31322*	31517*	31530*	31551
31193*	31305	31324	31518*	31533*	31552
31261	31306*	31326	31519*	31542	31553*
31263*					

4-4-0   D1 & E1   SECR

In order to produce a more powerful locomotive with a light axle load for use on the Chatham route to Dover on passenger trains Maunsell rebuilt eleven of Wainwright's E and twenty-one of his D class. The first E was modified in 1918 and after extensive trials the other ten followed. Rebuilding of the D class began in 1921 and was completed by the end of 1927. Both types were very similar after rebuilding and were quite often grouped as one class.

Some of the modifications made by Maunsell were the fitting of a larger superheated boiler, Belpaire firebox and long travel piston valves.

The first was withdrawn in 1944 (an air raid victim during the war) but the rest entered B.R. stock. Seventeen were still in service during the spring of 1960 but all were withdrawn by 1962.

Introduced	: 1918	Builder	: Rebuilt SECR & SR		
Pressure	: 180lb sq in	No. built	: 32		
Cylinders	: 19in x 26in	Weight	: 91tons 6cwt		
T.E.	: 17,951lb		93tons 1cwt*		
	18,411lb	Length	: 55ft		
Driving wheel	: 6ft 8in	Total	: 17		
	6ft 6in				
Bogie wheel	: 3ft 7in	E1*			

31019*	31246	31489	31505	31545	31739
31067*	31247	31491	31507*	31727	31749
31145	31487	31497*	31509	31735	

H class 0-4-4T No. 31276, Brighton, 5th June 1960 (push and pull fitted — note straight sided coal bunker).

D1 class 4-4-0 No. 31727, Ashford, 23rd March 1957.

0-6-0T   P   SECR

This class of miniature tank engines was introduced by Wainwright in February 1909 to replace the rather unsuccessful steam railmotors. Only eight were built and they were initially employed on auto-coach workings on the lightly trafficked lines such as Otford to Sevenoaks, Nunhead to Greenwich Park, Reading to Ash, Margate to Birchington, Westerham branch and the Isle of Sheppey Light Railway. They were not entirely successful and four were soon employed as light shunters or shed pilots. The remainder had their auto gear modified between December 1912 and July 1914 and were then returned to passenger working. However, this reprieve was short lived as all of the class were eventually relegated to shunting.

All eight survived to be taken into B.R. stock, but the first (31555) was withdrawn in 1955. Two more (31557 and 31178) followed in 1957/8, and one of these was sold to Bowaters for further use on their private railway. 31558 was withdrawn in February 1960 and 31325 in March leaving only three locomotives officially in traffic by spring of that year. 31323 was sold to the Bluebell Railway in June 1960 while 31556 went to Hodson's Mills that same year, leaving 31027 to be purchased by the Bluebell in 1961. It is interesting to note that two locomotives sold into industry have now been preserved.

Introduced	: 1909	Builder	:	S.E. & C.R.
Pressure	: 160lb sq in	No. built	:	8
Cylinders	: 12in x 18in	Weight	:	28tons 10cwt
T.E.	: 7,812lb	Length	:	24ft 1¾in
Driving wheel	: 3ft 9 1/8in	Total	:	3

31027   31323   31556

0-6-0   O1   SECR

Fifty-nine of the James Stirling's O class were modified between 1903 and 1932 and classified O1. They received new boilers with higher pressure in place of their Stirling domeless boilers, new cabs and a few other minor alterations.

Like the O class they were used almost exclusively on goods work. All but three engines survived until Nationalisation, but withdrawals accelerated during the 1950's, until only three remained in 1960. The last, 31065, was withdrawn in 1961 but later acquired for preservation.

Introduced	: 1903	Builder	:	Rebuilt SECR
Pressure	: 150lb sq in	No. built	:	59
Cylinders	: 18in x 26in	Weight	:	66tons 10cwt
T.E.	: 17,324lb	Total	:	3
	17,608lb*			
Driving wheel	: 5ft 2in			
	5ft 1in*			

31048*   31065   31258

P class 0-6-0T No. 31556, Brighton, 25th March 1961.

O1 class 0-6-0 No. 31065, Paddock Wood, 11th June 1961.

With goods train loadings increasing the small 0-6-0 types were finding it difficult to maintain schedules without resorting to double heading. Maunsell therefore designed and introduced a 2-6-0 which could be used equally well on goods or passenger workings. The prototype entered traffic in July 1917 but due to the war no further engines were constructed until 1920. No less than eighty-six were eventually built and the last entered traffic in January 1934.

At first they were allocated to the eastern section, but as more locomotives became available could be seen at Guildford, Salisbury and Bournemouth in increasing numbers. Later batches were forwarded to former L & S.W.R. territory, especially west of Exeter where they performed admirably on the hillier sections.

31407 to 31414 entered traffic fitted with smoke deflectors, but the rest of the class were similarly treated from 1934. Other minor modifications took place, including the fitting of U1 style chimneys on the earlier locomotives. After Nationalisation B.R. commenced fitting new cylinders with outside steam pipes, and since 1957 most of the re-cylindered and some original engines received a new design of blastpipe and chimney.

While the early N class were being constructed Maunsell decided to modify one of them by fitting a third cylinder. 31822 entered traffic in 1923 and the five later engines during 1930. Classified N1 they were allocated to eastern section sheds and frequently rostered on holiday trains from the metropolis to coastal resorts.

Both classes survived intact into the 1960's and withdrawals did not commence until 1962. All were out of traffic by the end of 1966.

Introduced	: 1917		Builder	: S.E.C.R. & S.R.	
Pressure	: 200lb sq in		No. built	: 86 (includes 6 N1)	
Cylinders	: 19in x 28in		Weight	. 100tons 9cwt	
	(3) 16in x 28in*			104tons 10cwt (approx)*	
T.E.	: 26,036lb, 27,695lb*		Length	: 57ft 10 in (approx)	
Driving wheel	: 5ft 6in		Total	: 86	
Bogie	: 3ft 1in				
			N1 class		

31400	31810	31825	31839	31853	31867
31401	31811	31826	31840	31854	31868
31402	31812	31827	31841	31855	31869
31403	31813	31828	31842	31856	31870
31404	31814	31829	31843	31857	31871
31405	31815	31830	31844	31858	31872
31406	31816	31831	31845	31859	31873
31407	31817	31832	31846	31860	31874
31408	31818	31833	31847	31861	31875
31409	31819	31834	31848	31862	31876*
31410	31820	31835	31849	31863	31877*
31411	31821	31836	31850	31864	31878*
31412	31822*	31837	31851	31865	31879*
31413	31823	31838	31852	31866	31880*
31414	31824				

N class 2-6-0 No 31831, Exmouth Junction, 18th April 1960.

N1 class 2-6-0 No. 31879, Tonbridge, 23rd March 1957.

In 1913 Maunsell prepared plans for a new powerful and beautifully proportioned express passenger tank locomotive for the S.E. & C.R. Though their construction was delayed due to the war, the first was ready for service by June 1917.

Designated K or 'River' class it had six foot driving wheels and was of the 2-6-4 wheel arrangement. Weighing 82tons 12cwt it was to all intents and purposes a large wheeled tank version of the N class, having identical boiler and cylinders.

In 1923 orders were placed for an additional twenty engines and these were delivered during 1925 and 1926. The last to be constructed was also modified in a similar manner to the N1 class and became the solitary three cylindered K1. They all received names after rivers in Southern Railway territory and were put to work on express passenger trains to Brighton, Eastbourne, Dover, Portsmouth and Reading. Unfortunately over a very short period four of the class left the track and one with serious consequences. They were all taken out of traffic in 1927 pending an enquiry.

It appeared that a few factors caused the engines to roll at speed, but the most significant was the poor condition of the track. Rather than have the whole class lying idle for a number of years while renewal of the permanent way was undertaken, it was decided to convert the River class into 2-6-0 tender engines.

The first was outshopped in March 1928 and the remainder during that same year. In their new guise they were designated U and U1.

Early in 1927 orders had been placed for additional River class tanks, but with the developments later in that year they were constructed as tender engines. By the end of 1929 there were forty of the class in service allocated to Guildford, Nine Elms, Eastbourne, Redhill and Reading. An additional ten were constructed at Ashford during 1931.

The solitary K1 re-entered traffic in June 1928 as a U1. However it was not to remain alone, as twenty similar engines were outshopped from Eastleigh during 1931.

The U and U1's received few modifications from 1931 to Nationalisation, though some locomotives were altered for experimental purposes. From 1954 new cylinders and outside steam pipes, similar to the N class, replaced the older style on a number of engines and also new chimneys from 1957.

All were in traffic during 1960 in the south east, Brighton, Bournemouth, Eastleigh and Yeovil areas, but gradually became withdrawn until extinct by 1966.

Introduced	:	1917 (as K class)	Builder	:	Rebuilt S.R.
Pressure	:	200lb sq in	No. built	:	71 (includes 21 U1)
Cylinders	:	19in x 28in	Weight	:	102tons 16cwt
		(3) 16in x 28in*			105tons 16cwt*
T.E.	:	23,866lb, 25,387lb*	Length	:	57ft 10 in (approx)
Driving wheel	:	6ft	Total	:	71
Bogie wheel	:	3ft 1in			
			U1 class *		

Rebuilt from K class with minor variations (including larger splashers)†
Rebuilt from K1 class with minor variations (including larger splashers)‡

U class 2-6-0 No. 31628, Feltham, 1st July 1961.

U class 2-6-0 No. 31804, Eastleigh, 4th May 1963 (rebuilt from River class tank — note larger splashers).

31610	31622	31634	31796†	31808†	31900*
31611	31623	31635	31797†	31809†	31901*
31612	31624	31636	31798†	31890*†	31902*
31613	31625	31637	31799†	31891*	31903*
31614	31626	31638	31800†	31892*	31904*
31615	31627	31639	31801†	31893*	31905*
31616	31628	31790†	31802†	31894*	31906*
31617	31629	31791†	31803†	31895*	31907*
31618	31630	31792†	31804†	31896*	31908*
31619	31631	31793†	31805†	31897*	31909*
31620	31632	31794†	31806†	31898*	31910*
31621	31633	31795†	31807†	31899*	

4-4-0   L & L1   SECR & SR

Introduced to cope with the increasing Continental traffic the L class was the largest locomotive permitted on certain main line sections of the S.E. & C.R. until the arrival of the Schools class. They all entered traffic in 1914 (twelve constructed by Beyer Peacock & Co. and ten by A. Borsig) and were originally allocated to Bricklayers Arms, Dover, Hastings and Cannon Street.

Maunsell was never completely satisfied with the design, and when the weight of trains increased he placed an order with the North British Loco. Co. for fifteen similar but greatly improved machines of the L1 class. They entered traffic in 1920 and differed by having smaller cylinders, long-travel valves, Maunsell superheater, higher boiler pressure, N smoke-boxes, standard chimneys and other cosmetic alterations.

The original L class was modified along similar lines between 1930 and 1944.

They remained almost exclusively in the South Eastern section although late in their life the few survivors were stationed at Nine Elms. The first was withdrawn in 1956 and all had gone by late 1962.

Introduced	: 1914	Builder	: Various	
Pressure	: 180lb sq in	No. built	: 37 (includes 15 L1)	
Cylinders	: 19½ in x 26in	Weight	: 97tons 15cwt	
T.E.	: 18,908lb		98tons 6cwt*	
Driving wheel	: 6ft 8in	Length	: 56ft 8in (approx.)	
Bogie wheel	: 3ft 7in	Total	: 19	

L1 class *

31753*	31759*	31764	31768	31780	31786*
31754*	31760	31765	31771	31782*	31787*
31756*	31763	31766	31776	31783*	31789*
31757*					

U1 class 2-6-0 No. 31907, Tonbridge, 10th June 1961.

L1 class 4-4-0 No. 31759, Ashford, 23rd March 1957.

2-6-4T   W   SR

Maunsell introduced the chunky W class tanks from January 1932 to handle transfer freight traffic across London. They were considered an improved tank version of the N and N1 series of tender engines. In all, fifteen were constructed by Eastleigh (5) and Ashford (10) workshops, the last not entering traffic until April 1936.

Although they were tried experimentally on some short distance passenger trains the W class remained almost exclusively in the London area. However, near the end of their lives a few saw service further afield.

All of the class entered British Railways stock and the last three survived until 1964.

Introduced	: 1932	Builder	: S.R.
Cylinders	: (3) 16½in x 28in	Pressure	: 200lb sq in
T.E.	: 29,452lb	No. built	: 15
Driving wheel	: 5ft 6in	Weight	: 90tons 14cwt
Bogie wheel	: 3ft 1in	Length	: 44ft ¼in
Trailing wheel	: 3ft 1in	Total	: 15

31911	31914	31917	31920	31922	31924
31912	31915	31918	31921	31923	31925
31913	31916	31919			

2-6-0   K   LBSCR

Introduced in September 1913 the K class moguls were initially used on some of the heaviest goods trains on the L.B.S.C.R. Designed by L.B. Billinton a total of seventeen were constructed over a nine year period.

Originally allocated to Brighton, Fratton and Norwood they spent most of their lives on the Brighton section, until withdrawn en bloc in 1962.

Introduced	: 1913	Builder	: L.B.S.C.R.
Pressure	: 180lb sq in	No. built	: 17
Cylinders	: 21in x 26in	Weight	: 105tons 5cwt
T.E.	: 26,580lb	Length	: 57ft 10in
Driving wheel	: 5ft 6in	Total	: 17
Bogie wheel	: 3ft 6in		

32337	32340	32343	32346	32349	32352
32338	32341	32344	32347	32350	32353
32339	32342	32345	32348	32351	

0-6-0   C2x   LBSCR

The C2x class freight engines were a rebuild by D. Earle Marsh of R.J. Billington's C2 class, introduced in 1893. Of the original fifty-five C2's all but ten were rebuilt between 1908 and 1940 with 5 foot diameter boilers, extended smokeboxes and higher pressure boilers.

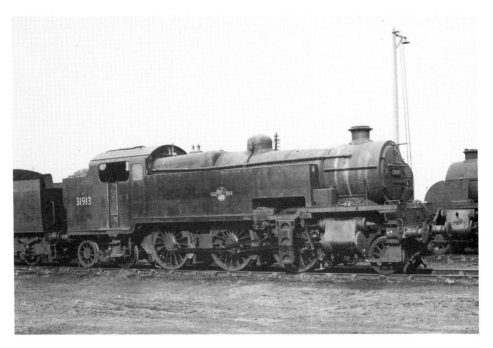

W class 2-6-4T No. 31913, Feltham, 8th March 1964.

K class 2-6-0 No. 32346, Brighton, 5th June 1960.

Some locomotives were fitted with a second dome between the original and the chimney. This was in conjunction with a feed water system, but it was later blanked off. The extra dome however remained.

The first of the original C2 class was withdrawn in 1935 and all had gone by 1950. Used mainly on the Brighton section, the first C2x was not withdrawn until 1957. The last was taken out of service during 1962.

Introduced	: 1908	Builder	: Vulcan		
Pressure	: 170lb sq in	No. built	: 45 (rebuilt)		
Cylinders	: 17½in x 26in	Weight	: 45tons 5cwt		
T.E.	: 19,176lb	Total	: 32		
Driving wheel	: 5ft				

32438	32449	32525	32535	32543	32548
32441	32450	32527	32536	32544	32549
32443	32451	32528	32538	32545	32550
32445	32521	32532	32539	32546	32552
32446	32522	32534	32541	32547	32553
32448	32523				

0-6-0T   E1   LBSCR

Introduced in 1874 no less than seventy-three of these sturdy goods tank engines were constructed at Brighton workshops under the direction of William Stroudley. In 1891 Billinton built a further six engines, but with detail differences. They were re-boilered by Marsh early this century with higher pressure boilers.

During 1927/8 ten of the class were rebuilt as 0-6-2T's, classified E1R, for use in the West Country. This increased their weight to 50 tons 5 cwt, but other dimensions remained unaltered. The first of this batch was withdrawn in 1955 and the last during 1959.

Four E1's were shipped to the Isle of Wight during 1932, renumbered W1 to W4, and named after localitites.

The first locomotive was withdrawn in 1908 but about thirty E1 class survived Nationalisation. Two lasted into the spring of 1960, but the last (32694) was withdrawn the following year.

One of the class (Southern Railway No. 110) was sold to the Cannock and Rugeley Colliery Company in April 1927. Renumbered 9 on their roster it was also given the name Cannock Wood and a new, but different, boiler was constructed and fitted by Bagnalls. It had an increased boiler pressure of 175lb sq in, which in turn gave it a higher tractive effort (19,106lb) than its sisters on the Southern. Withdrawn from service in 1963, No. 9 was sold for preservation and eventually purchased by four members of the East Somerset Railway. It arrived at Cranmore in September 1978 and will be restored as No. 32110 — a number it would have carried had it survived Nationalisation.

Introduced	: 1874	Builder	: L.B.S.C.R.
Pressure	: 170lb sq in	No. built	: 79
Cylinders	: 17in x 24in	Weight	: 44tons 3 cwt
T.E.	: 18,560lb	Length	: 32ft 4½in
Driving wheel	: 4ft 6in	Total	: 2

W4 Wroxall   32694

C2x class 0-6-0 No. 32527, Norwood Junction, 5th September 1959 (two domes).

E1 class 0-6-0T No. 32689, Eastleigh, 14th May 1960 (withdrawn).

0-6-0T   E2   LBSCR

The numerically small E2 class was constructed by L.B. Billinton to replace some of the earlier E1 series. They were placed in service in two batches during 1913 (100 to 104) and 1915/6 (105 to 109). The second batch differed by having extended upper sections to their side tanks*.

Used on light freight work and shunting all were taken into British Railways stock and the class remained intact until 1961. Withdrawals then continued and the remainder were taken out of traffic by the end of 1963.

Introduced	: 1913	Builder	: L.B.S.C.R.
Pressure	: 170lb sq in	No. built	: 10
Cylinders	: 17½in x 26in	Weight	: 52tons 15cwt
T.E.	: 21,307lb		53tons 10cwt*
Driving wheel	: 4ft 6in	Total	: 10

32100	32102	32104	32106	32108	32109
32101	32103	32105	32107		

0-6-2T   E4   LBSCR

Built in considerable numbers from 1897 the E4 class were designed to handle the London suburban passenger traffic. With 5 foot drivers they were a variation of the earlier E3 goods tanks of which none survived into the 1960's.

Four of the class were modified with higher pressure boilers between 1909 and 1912 but no others were so treated. Classified E4x these variants were all withdrawn by 1959.

With the expanding electrification program a large number of E4's became redundant and some were refurbished and transferred to former L & S.W.R. territory to replace the smaller G6 class.

The first of the class was withdrawn in 1944, but the rest remained active until 1955. All were out of traffic by 1963, but one engine (32473) was sold to Bluebell Railway in October 1962 for preservation. It reverted to its Brighton number of 473 and its former name of *Birch Grove* was painted on the side tanks.

Introduced	: 1897	Builder	: L.B.S.C.R.
Pressure	: 160lb sq in	No. built	: 75
Cylinders	: 17½in x 26in	Weight	: 57tons 10cwt
T.E.	: 18,048lb	Length	: 35ft 3in
Driving wheel	: 5ft	Total	: 32

32468	32475	32498	32506	32556	32564
32469	32479	32500	32509	32557	32565
32470	32484	32503	32510	32559	32578
32472	32487	32504	32512	32562	32580
32473	32491	32505	32515	32563	32581
32474	32495				

E2 class 0-6-0T No. 32109, Eastleigh, 4th May 1963 (extended tanks).

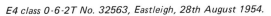

E4 class 0-6-2T No. 32563, Eastleigh, 28th August 1954.

0-6-2T   E6   LBSCR

Another development by Billinton of the series of 0-6-2 tanks designed for light freight and shunting work, the E6's, were built during 1904 and 1905. The class consisted of only twelve locomotives, of which two were rebuilt as E6x (higher pressure boilers) during 1911, but withdrawn prior to 1960.

By the mid 1950's they were allocated to Norwood Junction and Bricklayers Arms depots. Withdrawals commenced in 1957 and all were out of traffic by the end of 1962.

Introduced	: 1904	Builder	: L.B.S.C.R.
Pressure	: 160lb sq in	No. built	: 12
Cylinders	: 18in x 26in	Weight	: 61tons
T.E.	: 21,216lb	Trailing wheel	: 4ft
Driving wheel	: 4ft 6in	Total	: 6

32408	32410	32415	32416	32417	32418

0-6-0T   A1 & A1x   LBSCR

One of the most famous of all tank classes in the British Isles the A1, or 'Terriers' as they are more affectionately known, were some of the oldest engines in service on British Railways. Based on William Stroudley's earlier design for the Highland Railway, they were introduced on the L.B.S.C.R. in 1872, for lighter suburban passenger work. A total of fifty were constructed between 1872 and 1880.

Train loads gradually increased and by the turn of the century these diminutive engines were finding it hard to cope. Subsequently a number were sent to country outposts for branch line work, while some were sold to private Industry and others to pre grouping railways. A few locomotives later found their way to the Isle of Wight and at least four spent time in Departmental stock. As it would be impossible to completely cover the wanderings of the locomotives in such a small volume the above will have to suffice.

Seventeen of the A1 class were reboilered, the most noticeable feature being extended smokeboxes, and classified A1x around the 1910 to 1915 period. Other alterations included the fitting of push and pull apparatus.

In 1948 one A1 class and fourteen A1x's were taken into stock by B.R., while an additional A1 (82 *Boxhill*) was withdrawn from service in 1946 but retained for preservation. In the spring of 1960 eleven A1x and one A1 were still in service. Their last duties were working the Hayling Island branch, but with its closure in November 1963 they were finally made redundant. However, this was not the end of their careers as railway preservation was beginning to blossom, and their suitability for light branch lines made them much sought after. In all, ten of a total of fifty locomotives are now preserved, either in working order or as static exhibits.

Introduced	: 1872	Builder	: L.B.S.C.R.
Pressure	: 150lb sq in	No. built	: 50
Cylinders	: 12in x 20in	Weight	: 27tons 10cwt†
	14 $3/16$in x 20in*		28tons 5cwt

E6 class 0-6-2T No. 32408, Feltham, 5th March 1961.

A1x class 0-6-0T No. 32650, Havant, 3rd August 1959.

T.E.	: 7,650lb	Length	: 26ft ½in
	10,693lb*	Total	: 12
Driving wheel	: 4ft	*A1†*	

| 32635 | 32640 | 32650 | 32661 | 32670 | DS680† |
| 32636* | 32646 | 32655 | 32662 | 32678 | DS681 |

0-6-0   Q1   SR

To assist with the anticipated increase of freight traffic on the Southern due to the hostilities in Europe Bulleid received authority to construct a class of forty powerful freight engines. After much consideration he finally opted for a completely new and rather unconventional looking 0-6-0 which had the largest possible boiler and greatest route availability rather than perpetuate, or modify, a tried design. With material shortages this new locomotive was truly an austerity, being devoid of footplate, splashers and other such luxuries.

The class leader entered traffic in March 1942, followed by the other thirty-nine that same year. They were numbered C1 to C40 by Bulleid as part of his new European style numbering system and were initially allocated to Guildford, Eastleigh and Feltham.

Despite a number of design compromises they proved very successful and reliable machines, with few necessary modifications over the years.

Withdrawals did not commence until 1963 when thirteen were taken out of traffic. This was followed by another twenty in 1964 and four in 1965. The remaining three (33006/20/27) were withdrawn in January 1966, but No. 33001 was retained for preservation as part of the National collection.

Introduced	: 1942	Builder	: S.R.
Pressure	: 230lb sq in	No. built	: 40
Cylinders	: 19in x 26in	Weight	: 89tons 5cwt
T.E.	: 30,081lb	Length	: 54ft 10½in
Driving wheel	: 5ft 1in	Total	: 40

33001	33008	33015	33022	33029	33035
33002	33009	33016	33023	33030	33036
33003	33010	33017	33024	33031	33037
33004	33011	33018	33025	33032	33038
33005	33012	33019	33026	33033	33039
33006	33013	33020	33027	33034	33040
33007	33014	33021	33028		

4-6-2   WC & BB   SR

From a proposed 2-6-0 replacement locomotive for the ageing T9 class in the West Country Oliver Bulleid evolved a handsome lightweight Pacific based on his controversial Merchant Navy class. Incorporating many of the new features such as Bulleid-Firth Brown Pattern wheels, thermic syphons, wide Belpair firebox, Lemaitre blastpipe, high 280lb sq in boiler pressure, valve-gear enclosed in an oil bath, and air smoothed casing, they looked indeed like a Merchant Navy.

Q1 class 0-6-0 No. 33018, Feltham, 29th May 1960.

Unrebuilt WC class 4-6-2 No. 34035 Shaftestbury, Eastleigh, 2nd June 1963.

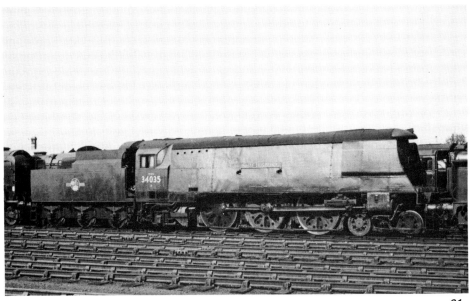

The first of the class (21C101 *Exeter*) was outshopped from Brighton in May 1945, closely followed by others of the initial batch of twenty. A further thirty-two entered traffic in 1946, and eighteen in 1947. The remaining engines, numbered 34071 to 34110, were issued to traffic between 1948 and 1951, under British Railways ownership and as such never carried the number allotted by Bulleid.

After initial running in trials in the Brighton area most of them were transferred to the West Country and named after towns, cities and geographical locations. Later locomotives, designated Battle of Britain class, were built with minor modifications and named after Royal Air Force Squadrons. Both classes could be found working over most lines of the former Southern Railway.

Bulleid's chain driven valve gear enclosed in an oil bath had always been a controversial feature and after the successful rebuilding of some Merchant Navies along more conventional lines it was decided to similarly modify a number of these smaller Pacifics. In May 1957 the first rebuilt West Country, No. 34005, appeared minus its air smoothed casing and with Walschaerts valve gear. A total of seventy-five were scheduled for reconstruction but, because of the short life expectancy of steam traction, this was later reduced to sixty, the last being treated in May 1961.

A number of other modifications took place to both the originals and rebuilds, and one of particular note was the fitting of Giesl ejector to No. 34064 in May 1962. It seemed a rather pointless exercise as the decision to replace steam had been made some years earlier.

Bulleid's light Pacifics were magnificent to watch in action, especially with maximum tonnage in tow. Although capable of much heavier tasks they could also be found on short stopping trains.

The first of the class was officially withdrawn in April 1963, but a larger number lingered until the end of steam on the Southern. Fortunately examples of both rebuilt and original locomotives have been preserved.

Introduced	: 1945	Builder	: S.R.
Pressure	: 250lb sq in	No. built	: 110
Cylinders	: (3) 16 3/8 in x 24 in	Weight	: 128tons 12cwt (min)
T.E.	: 27,719lb		138tons (approx)*
Driving wheel	: 6ft 2in	Length	: 67ft 4¾in
Bogie wheel	: 3ft 1in	Total	: 110
Trailing wheel	: 3ft 1in		

Rebuilt *, Battle of Britain class †

34001	Exeter*	34013	Okehampton*
34002	Salisbury	34014	Budleigh Salterton*
34003	Plymouth*	34015	Exmouth*
34004	Yeovil*	34016	Bodmin*
34005	Barnstaple*	34017	Ilfracombe*
34006	Bude	34018	Axminster*
34007	Wadebridge	34019	Bideford
34008	Padstow*	34020	Seaton
34009	Lyme Regis*	34021	Dartmoor*
34010	Sidmouth*	34022	Exmoor*
34011	Tavistock	34023	Blackmore Vale
34012	Launceston*	34024	Tamar Valley*

Unrebuilt WC class 4-6-2 No. 34006 Bude, Eastleigh, 26th March 1966 (extended smoke deflectors).

Rebuilt WC class 4-6-2 No. 34036 Westward Ho, Eastleigh, 2nd June 1963.

34025	Whimple*	34068	Kenley†
34026	Yes Tor*	34069	Hawkinge†
34027	Taw Valley*	34070	Manston†
34028	Eddystone*	34071	601 Squadron†*
34029	Lundy*	34072	257 Squadron†
34030	Watersmeet	34073	249 Squadron†
34031	Torrington*	34074	46 Squadron†
34032	Camelford*	34075	264 Squadron†
34033	Chard	34076	41 Squadron†
34034	Honiton*	34077	603 Squadron†*
34035	Shaftesbury	34078	222 Squadron†
34036	Westward Ho*	34079	141 Squadron†
34037	Clovelly*	34080	74 Squadron†
34038	Lynton	34081	92 Squadron†
34039	Boscastle*	34082	615 Squadron†*
34040	Crewkerne*	34083	605 Squadron†
34041	Wilton	34084	253 Squadron†
34042	Dorchester*	34085	501 Squadron†*
34043	Coombe Martin	34086	219 Squadron†
34044	Woolacombe*	34087	145 Squadron†*
34045	Ottery St. Mary*	34088	213 Squadron†*
34046	Braunton*	34089	602 Squadron†*
34047	Callington*	34090	Sir Eustace Missenden, Southern
34048	Crediton*		Railway†*
34049	Anti-Aircraft Command†	34091	Weymouth
34050	Royal Observer Corps†*	34092	City of Wells
34051	Winston Churchill†	34093	Saunton*
34052	Lord Dowding†*	34094	Mortehoe
34053	Sir Keith Park†*	34095	Brentor*
34054	Lord Beaverbrook†	34096	Trevone*
34055	Fighter Pilot†	34097	Holsworthy*
34056	Croydon†*	34098	Templecombe*
34057	Biggin Hill†	34099	Lynmouth
34058	Sir Frederick Pile†*	34100	Appledore*
34059	Sir Archibald Sinclair†*	34101	Hartland*
34060	25 Squadron†*	34102	Lapford
34061	73 Squadron†	34103	Calstock
34062	17 Squadron†*	34104	Bere Alston*
34063	229 Squadron†	34105	Swanage
34064	Fighter Command†	34106	Lydford
34065	Hurricane†	34107	Blandford Forum
34066	Spitfire†	34108	Wincanton*
34067	Tangmere†	34109	Sir Trafford Leigh-Mallory†*
		34110	66 Squadron†

4-6-2   **MN**   **SR**

When Oliver Bulleid took the reigns as Chief Mechanical Engineer of the Southern Railway, he inherited some rather run down locomotives. This was no reflection on his predecessor but more a portrayal of the general attitude to steam power by the Southern Railway management. Electrification was flourishing, at the expense of the ageing steam fleet.

Unrebuilt WC class 4-6-2 No 34002 Salisbury, Wadebridge, 27th July 1963.

Rebuilt BB class 4-6-2 No. 34053 Sir Keith Park, near Brockenhurst, 14th September 1963.

Bulleid believed in steam propulsion and he was eager to prove that it could be made a more viable proposition by adopting features alien to British Locomotive practise.

An obvious diplomat he managed to convince the Southern Railway Board that there was a need for a new express locomotive. He duly received authorisation for twenty, but later managed to increase the order to thirty locomotives of an unspecified design.

After considering the alternatives of conventional steam types and even eight coupled engines he settled on a Pacific. With the growing hostilities in Europe and subsequent material problems he classified his new locomotive as a mixed traffic type to enable production to continue during the war years.

The first of the 'Merchant Navy' class was outshopped from Eastleigh in February 1941 and after various tests and road trials entered traffic in June that same year. It was radically different from normal S.R. practise, with its air smoothed slab sided casing, high 280 lb sq in boiler pressure, revolutionary chain driven valve gear, all steel welded firebox, thermic syphons, steam reversing gear and BFB pattern wheels.

With Britain's involvement in the European crisis, only ten locomotives received the final sanction and these were built during 1941-42, numbered 21C1 to 21C10. However, Bulleid persuaded the board to permit the construction of a further ten and they were outshopped between December 1944 and June 1945. The remaining locomotives entered service under British Railways ownership between September 1948 and April 1949, never carrying Bulleid's numbers.

There were naturally a number of teething problems and one which received much adverse publicity was the leaking of oil from the valve gear casing. This was believed to accentuate the Merchant Navy's tendency to slip, but also, when the oil worked its way onto the boiler lagging, could cause the engine to catch fire. Modifications were made to the original design during 1942-43 but this made little apparent change. 21C6 was fitted with a re-designed casing in April 1944 and this greatly reduced leaking.

During the war years various tests were undertaken to improve the smoke deflecting effectiveness of the front casing. Eventually the familiar pattern front end (as illustrated in the photograph of 35002) was adopted as it tunnelled enough draught to sufficiently lift the smoke clear of the driver's cabin.

Other modifications were undertaken over the years, but due to their continued high coal consumption and repair costs in particular, a decision had to be made on their future. In the early 1950's British Railways were faced with two alternatives, either scrap the whole class and replace them with the new Standard Britannias, or institute a complete rebuilding program. Fortunately the latter was chosen, and between 1956 and 1959 all thirty were transformed into a more orthodox locomotive with Walschaerts valve gear and the air smoothed casing was discarded. In their new guise they acquitted themselves admirably and were unequalled in performance, economy and speed (despite their 'mixed traffic' 6ft 2in diameter driving wheels).

The Merchant Navies were used on the most prestigeous and heaviest passenger trains on the Southern. They were allocated, during the mid 1950's, to such sheds as Nine Elms, Bournemouth, Exmouth Junction, Salisbury and Stewarts Lane.

Withdrawals did not commence until 1964, when the Western Region began its dieselisation of the main line to Exeter. 35001/2/6/9/15/18 and 25 were all withdrawn that year, while the remainder were working from Bournemouth, Salisbury and Weymouth depots.

MN class 4-6-2 No. 35002 Union Castle, Nine Elms, 21st September 1957 (before rebuilding)

MN class 4-6-2 No. 35030 Elder-Dempster Lines (minus nameplates), Weymouth, 10th June 1967.

Withdrawals continued slowly until by November 1966 only ten remained. Seven survived until the end of steam, nos. 35003/7/8/13/23/28 and 30, and they worked regular services on the Weymouth to Waterloo lines as well as a number of special excursions elsewhere. They were all withdrawn in July 1967, the end of Southern Region steam in regular traffic.

35028 was purchased for preservation when withdrawn on 9th July 1967, but others have since been rescued from Barry scrapyard.

Introduced	: 1941	Builder	: S.R.	
Pressure	: 250lb sq in	No. built	: 30	
Cylinders	: (3) 18in x 24in	Weight	: 149tons (average)	
T.E.	: 33,495lb	Length	: 69ft 7¾in	
Driving wheel	: 6ft 2in	Trailing wheel	: 3ft 7in	
Bogie wheel	: 3ft 1in	Total	: 30	

35001	Channel Packet	35016	Elders Fyffes
35002	Union Castle	35017	Belgian Marine
35003	Royal Mail	35018	British India Line
35004	Cunard White Star	35019	French Line C.G.T.
35005	Canadian Pacific	35020	Bibby Line
35006	Peninsular & Orient S.N. Co.	35021	New Zealand Line
35007	Aberdeen Commonwealth	35022	Holland-America Line
35008	Orient Line	35023	Holland-Afrika Line
35009	Shaw Savill	35024	East Asiatic Company
35010	Blue Star	35025	Brocklebank Line
35011	General Steam Navigation	35026	Lamport & Holt Line
35012	United States Lines	35027	Port Line
35013	Blue Funnel	35028	Clan Line
35014	Nederland Line	35029	Ellerman Lines
35015	Rotterdam Lloyd	35030	Elder-Dempster Lines

0-4-0T   C14   LSWR

Drummond introduced a batch of small 2-2-0 tank engines from 1906 for railmotor working. They were not entirely successful and were soon found on shunting duties. Four were rebuilt to an 0-4-0T between 1913 and 1923, with three entering British Railways stock. 30588 and 30589 were both withdrawn in 1957 but the third had been transferred to departmental stock much earlier and could be found shunting at Redbridge sleeper depot, near Southampton, until withdrawn around 1960.

Introduced	: 1906	Builder	: L & S.W.R.
Pressure	: 150lb sq in	No. built	: 10
Cylinders	: 14in x 14in	Weight	: 25tons 15cwt
T.E.	: 9,718lb	Length	: 19ft 7in
Driving wheel	: 3ft	Total	: 1

77s

With the Electrification of the railway to Bournemouth regular steam workings on the Southern ceased on the 9th July 1967.

Nameplate of MN class No. 35008.

C14 class 0-4-0T No. 30589 (withdrawn 1957), Southampton Docks, 15th August 1951.

The last R1 class was withdrawn just prior to Spring 1960 and is therefore not featured in this book. A few were fitted with a short chimney and original cab for working the Canterbury and Whitstable line, and through a tunnel with very limited clearance at Tylers Hill. No. 31010 was one of this group pictured at Ashford, 1st August 1959.

Another class that disappeared even earlier was the Drummond D15 class 4-4-0's. The few survivors were finally replaced by the U class 2-6-0's and all were withdrawn by early 1956. No. 30465 was pictured at Waterloo on the 28th August 1954, 18 months before being withdrawn.

A1 class 0-6-0T No. DS680, Eastleigh, 24th March 1963. It was the last A1 in traffic, although in Departmental stock.

SECR L class 4-4-0 No. 31768 at Eastleigh workshops with a special train, 18th September 1960.

A1x class 0-6-0T No. 32670, Eastleigh, 18th May 1963.
M7 class 0-4-4T No. 30032, Feltham, 5th March 1961.